# Dwight L. Moody Instruction Book

*A Classic Treasury of*
*Timeless Wisdom and Reflection*

Tulsa, Oklahoma

Scripture quotations are taken from the *King James Version* of the Bible.

*Dwight L. Moody's Little Instruction Book*
*A Classic Treasury of Timeless Wisdom and Reflection*
ISBN 1-56292-049-9
Copyright © 1996 by Honor Books, Inc.
P.O. Box 55388
Tulsa, Oklahoma 74155

# ⌒ Introduction ⌒

During his lifetime (1837-99) Dwight L. Moody was one of America's most well-known and beloved evangelists. He became a Christian as an uneducated shoe salesman in Boston, Massachusetts. Immediately, he wanted to help the young street urchins who knew nothing of the love of God. From these humble beginnings, he was used by God as an instrument for revival — first in Chicago, then throughout the United States and Great Britain.

To truly be a Christian, Moody preached that every person must make the decision to receive Jesus Christ as their personal Lord and Savior. His message emphasized the love of God and the power of the Holy Spirit to renew the soul. By his personal example and teaching the Bible, he continually urged laypeople to influence the eternal destiny of unbelievers around them.

It has been estimated Moody preached to over one hundred million people during his lifetime, with an impact that extends to our day. His Moody Bible Institute has trained thousands of Christian workers, while various publishing channels he instituted continue to reach untold numbers with the Bible and great Christian literature.

In this *Little Instruction Book* you will see how Moody's down-to-earth, practical wit, and wisdom continue to reach our hearts today. He still challenges us to introduce others to Jesus, and encourages us to pursue a deeper relationship with Him.

Note: All quotes are by Dwight L. Moody unless indicated otherwise.

# GOD'S LOVE THAWS THE HEART

*"I never knew up to that time that God loved us so much. This heart of mine began to thaw out; I could not keep back the tears. I just drank it in ...I tell you there is one thing that draws above everything else in the world and that is love."*

## Restored Beauty

"[Our soul is] like a beautiful likeness that has been marred, daubed all over with streaks of black, and then restored to its full beauty of color when it is washed with the blood of Jesus Christ."

*How much more shall
the blood of Christ...
purge your conscience from
dead works to serve the living God?*
HEBREWS 9:14

## *DID YOU KNOW?*

When Moody was four years old, his father died,
leaving his mother, Betsy, to raise nine children
under the age of thirteen. She never encouraged
young Dwight to be educated or read the Bible.
He left home at seventeen to become a shoe salesman.

# IDOLS AT HOME

"*You don't have to go to heathen lands today to find false gods, America is full of them. Whatever you love more than God is your idol.*"

## POWER IN THE PULPIT AND PEW

"Two or three men stood up and said, 'We had a new minister last Sunday—the same old minister, but he had got new power,'…We want new ministers in the pulpit and new people in the pews. We want people quickened by the Spirit of God."

"Some Christians have a very small Savior, for they are not willing to receive Him fully, and let Him do great and mighty things for them."

## A Small Savior?

*The eyes of your understanding being enlightened; that ye may know...what is the exceeding greatness of his power to us-ward who believe.*

EPHESIANS 1:18,19

## MEN, NOT MACHINES

*"Some say, 'If God loves me, why does He not make me good?' He does not want machines or slaves. He could break our stubborn hearts, but He wants to draw us toward Himself by the cords of love."*

# RELIGIOUS DECEPTION

*"Temptations are never so dangerous as when they come to us in a religious garb."*

## THE PERFECT GUIDE

"I am told by people who have been over the Alps, that if they are passing a dangerous place, they are fastened to the guide. The Christian should be linked to his unerring Guide, and be safely upheld."

# CHRIST HIMSELF IS THE ANSWER

"A man said: 'If you can answer these questions satisfactorily, I have made up my mind to become a Christian.' 'Do you not think you should come to Christ first?' After he had received Christ, he looked again at his list of questions; but...they had all been answered."

*Bothering God*

"Some people think God does not like to be troubled with our constant coming and asking. The only way to trouble God is not to come at all."

———

*...yet ye have not, because ye ask not.*

JAMES 4:2

# FALSE BACKSLIDERS

*"Some…claim to be backsliders, but they never have 'slid forward.' They may talk of backsliding, but they have never really been born again."*

## *DID YOU KNOW?*

When Moody first came to Chicago, he wanted to be a businessman and make $100,000.

# SOMETIMES IT DEPENDS ON YOU

*"There is no use asking God to do things you can do yourself."*

# FRESH EXPERIENCES

"*Do not expect the same experience that you had two or twenty years ago. You will have a fresh experience, and God will deal with you in His own way.*"

## A Square Bible?

"You can't destroy the Bible!
It is like a cube!
Every time you turn it over
it comes right side up!"

---

*The grass withereth,
the flower fadeth:
but the word of our God
shall stand for ever.*

ISAIAH 40:8

# THE LIGHT OF HUMILITY

*"Some people talk of how humble they are; [but] a lighthouse does not have a trumpet blown, it is its own witness."*

# THE PRIVILEGE OF THE SPIRIT

*"God commands us to be filled with the Spirit;
and if we aren't filled, it's because
we're living beneath our privileges."*

## A ROOT OF BITTERNESS

"*If we allow the root of bitterness, our prayer will not be answered. It may not be an easy thing to live in sweet fellowship with [everyone]; but that is what the grace of God is for.*"

## COLD AND DEAD

*"There are too many religious meetings
which are sadder than a funeral.
They breed people with faces bearing an expression
as chilling as an east blast from the lake."*

# GOD'S WILL FIRST

"After we have made our requests known to Him,
our language should be, 'Thy will be done.'
I would a thousand times rather that
God's will should be done than my own."

## SIN BLOCKS THE PROMISES

"I *sometimes tremble when I hear people quote promises, and say that God is bound to fulfill them, when all the time there is some sin in their lives they are not willing to give up.*"

### *DID YOU KNOW?*

Emma Revell, later to become Moody's wife, was the daughter of Fleming H. Revell, founder of a Christian publishing venture still in operation as of this writing.

# PRAYER OVER PREACHING

"We are not told that Jesus ever taught His disciples how to preach, but He taught them how to pray. He wanted them to have power with God; then He knew they would have power with man."

"Don't let the scoffers laugh you into hell;
they cannot laugh you out of it."

## Hell Isn't Funny

*Why do the heathen rage,
and the people imagine a vain thing?
He that sitteth in the heavens
shall laugh: the Lord shall
have them in derision.*

PSALM 2:1,4

## TRUE HOLINESS

"When we hear men trying to make out that they are holy, and speaking about their holiness, they make light of the holiness of God."

# THE SANDS OF TIME

*"Seeking to perpetuate one's name on earth is like writing on the sand by the seashore; to be perpetual it must be written on eternal shores."*

## QUALIFIED FOR SERVICE

*"If we have not grace enough for service, we have no one to blame but ourselves. He has [an] abundance of grace to qualify us to work for Him."*

## Little Things Count Big

"There are many of us that are willing to do great things for the Lord, but few of us are willing to do little things."

---

*But he that is greatest among you shall be your servant.*

MATTHEW 23:11

# MAKE ROOM FOR THE SPIRIT

"*If we are full of pride and conceit
and ambition and the world,
there is no room for the Spirit of God.*"

## A FATHER'S LOVE

*"After I became a father, and for years had an only son, it seemed to me as if it required more love for the Father to give His Son than for the Son to die."*

## DID YOU KNOW?

Presidents Lincoln and Grant
visited Moody's ministry.

## THE END RESULT

"There are many who make a profession of Christianity who fall away. It may be that those who seemed to promise the fairest turn out the worst, and those who did not promise so well turn out best in the end."

## Give Up the Little Blighters

"God does not call upon us to give up a single thing that adds to our happiness; all He wants us to give up are the things which are the blight of our lives."

---

*And if thine eye offend thee, pluck it out, and cast it from thee: it is better for thee to enter into life with one eye, rather than having two eyes to be cast into hell fire.*

MATTHEW 18:9

## GLORY BEYOND

"*Why should we go reeling and staggering
under the burdens and cares of life
when we have such prospects before us?
If there is nothing but glory beyond,
our faces ought to shine brightly all the time.*"

## *DID YOU KNOW?*

Moody brought the Gospel to soldiers
in the Civil War.

## HEAVENLY FIRE

"Have you ever passed through the furnace and been taught by the Spirit of God that your natural gifts go for naught unless you have the fire of heaven in your soul? You can't go on heavenly missions without heavenly fire."

"I know the Bible is inspired
because it inspires me."

## Personal Inspiration

*Thy word is a lamp
unto my feet,
and a light unto my path.*
PSALM 119:105

# FEEDING ON LOVE

"*I took up that word Love, and I do not know how many weeks I spent in studying the passages in which it occurs, till at last I could not help loving people. I had been feeding on love so long that I was anxious to do everybody good I came in contact with.*"

# TRUE BOLDNESS

"Peter was noted for his boldness, and a little maid scared him nearly out of his wits…He swore that he didn't know Christ…I'd like to have been there on the day of Pentecost alongside of that maid when she saw Peter preaching."

"The best way to revive a church, is to build a fire in the pulpit."

## Fire Where It Counts

Now when they saw the boldness of Peter and John, and perceived that they were unlearned and ignorant men, they marvelled; and they took knowledge of them, that they had been with Jesus.

ACTS 4:13

## JUSTIFIED BY GOD

"*Justification means that there isn't a charge against you. Your sins are completely wiped out; God says He puts them out of His memory.*"

# HIDDEN CHARACTER

*"Character is what you are in the dark."*

# THE GREAT WHITE THRONE

*"People live in constant dread of the Great White Throne Judgment. When that comes, I am going to be with Christ on the throne; I am not going to be judged!"*

# REFLECTIONS OF HEAVEN

*"A humble saint looks most
like a citizen of heaven."*

*The Christian Classics Series*

## DID YOU KNOW?

Moody's revival meetings helped
create relief programs for the poor.

# THE WILLS AND THE WONT'S

*"The elect are the 'whosoever wills;' the non-elect are the 'whosoever won'ts.'"*

# THE ROOTS OF RESPECT

"*Obedience and respect at home prepare the way for obedience to the employer, and they are joined with other virtues that help toward a prosperous career, crowned with a ripe, honored old age. Disrespect for parents are often the first steps in the downward track.*"

## *How To Make a Monster*

"If a man has a shriveled-up heart and a big head he is a monster."

———————

*Pride goeth before destruction, and an haughty spirit before a fall.*

PROVERBS 16:18

# MOUNTAINS OF SMOKE

"*The devil's mountains are only made of smoke. He can throw a straw into your path and make a mountain of it. He says to you, 'You cannot confess to your family; why, you'll break down'!...But when you accept Christ, you will have power to confess Him.*"

## A CHILD'S UNDERSTANDING

*"Would Christ have made a child the standard of faith if He had known that it was not capable of understanding His words?"*

## STUDYING HIS WORD

"The best law for Bible study is the law of
perseverance. The psalmist says, 'I have stuck
unto thy testimonies'....Some people are
like express trains; they skim along
so quickly that they see nothing."

## MIRRORS DON'T LIE

"*Some people wonder why their children are such liars. If they'd look into a mirror they'd probably see the reason.*"

# GO AGAINST THE FLOW

*"I thought when I became a Christian I had nothing to do but just to lay my oars in the bottom of the boat and float along. But I soon found that I would have to go against the current."*

## *DID YOU KNOW?*

Moody's own house burned down twice and his Chicago YMCA building burned three times.

## OVERCOMING THE WORLD

*"Love of the world means the forgetfulness of the eternal future by reason of love for passing things. How can the world be overcome? Not by education, not by experience; only by faith."*

## THE FLOOD COMMITTEE

*"If there had been a committee appointed,
Noah's ark would never have been built."*

# FAITH IN CHRIST ALONE

"It is not to have faith in this church, this doctrine, or that man, but it is to have faith in the man Christ Jesus at the right hand of God. That is the only faith that will ever save a soul."

## When I Am Weak

"Real true faith is man's weakness leaning on God's strength."

---

*Finally, my brethren,*
*be strong in the Lord,*
*and in the power of his might.*

EPHESIANS 6:10

# WORKING ON THE SABBATH

"A Christian man was once urged by his employer to work on Sunday. 'Does not your Bible say that if your ass falls into a pit on the Sabbath, you may pull him out?' 'Yes,' replied the other; 'but if the ass had the habit of falling into the same pit every Sabbath, I would either fill up the pit or sell the ass.'"

# DO ONE THING WELL

*"Give me a man who says, 'This one thing I do.' and not, 'These fifty things, I dabble in.'"*

## THE LAST TRUMPET

"The ears that will not obey the sound of the churchgoing bell will be compelled to obey the sound of the last trumpet. The eyes that behold evil here shall one day gaze upon the spotless throne of God. Do not forever disobey."

## Instant Salvation

"I believe a man may be as vile
as hell itself one moment
and be saved the next."

---

*And it shall come to pass, that
whosoever shall call on the name of
the Lord shall be saved.*

ACTS 2:21

## OBEDIENCE IN HEAVEN

"A *Sunday School teacher once asked her class, 'How is the will of God done in heaven?' One child answered, 'Cheerfully.' Another, 'By everybody.' A third, 'All the time.' But the best answer was, 'It is done without asking any questions.'"*

# THE OTHER SIDE OF CALVARY

*"We ought in these days to have far more faith than Abel or Enoch or Abraham had…They lived in the dim light of the past, while we are in the full blaze of Calvary and the resurrection."*

## *DID YOU KNOW?*

Though Moody completed only the equivalent of the fifth grade, he started three institutions of higher education still thriving today: Moody Bible Institute, Mount Herman Academy, and Northfield Academy.

## *DID YOU KNOW?*

Moody was responsible for two Christian publishing companies still serving the cause of the Gospel: Moody Press and Fleming H. Revell.

The reward of service is more service.

---

## It's Own Reward

*For unto whomsoever much is given,
of him shall be much required:
and to whom men
have committed much,
of him they will ask the more.*

LUKE 12:48

## EXAMPLES TO OUR CHILDREN

"*Have you lived so godly and so Christlike a life that you can say, 'Follow me as I follow Christ?' Are your children walking in wisdom? Are their names written in the Lamb's Book of Life? How many fathers and mothers today would be able to answer yes?*"

## PRIMING THE PUMP

*"Lots of Christians are like the old farmer's pump — pretty good pump except when it was either dried up or froze up."*

## AN EASY MASTER

*"I have been in this school for forty years, and I want to testify that I have found an easy master. I used to say, as you do, 'It is a hard thing to be a Christian,' and I thought it was; but now I tell you that the yoke is easy and the burden light."*

# PRAYER'S PROPER LENGTH

"A *man who prays much in private*
*will make short prayers in public."*

## FORGIVEN FREELY

"There is no father on earth who has as much love in his heart as God has for you. You may be sinful as hell; yet God stands ready and willing to receive you to His bosom and to forgive you freely."

## NO MORE STING

"*Take a hornet and pluck the sting out;
you are not afraid of it after that any more
than of a fly. So death has lost its sting…
and I can look on death as a crushed victim.*"

## Walking the Walk

*For our gospel came not unto you in word only, but also in power, and in the Holy Ghost, and in much assurance; as ye know what manner of men we were among you for your sake.*

1 THESSALONIANS 1:5

## *DID YOU KNOW?*

Out of Moody's revival meetings at Cambridge University in England came the "Cambridge Seven," who were influential missionaries to China. Included in this group was C. T. Studd.

# THE GROWTH OF SIN

*"It would be easier to find a man that had not done any one sin than to find a man who had done it only once. Sin multiplies. We must either overcome sin, or it will overcome us."*

# THE BEAUTY OF HOLINESS

*"Next to the might of God, the serene beauty of a holy life is the most powerful influence for good in all the world."*

# THE GLORIOUS FANATIC

*"I suppose they say of me, 'He is a radical;
he is a fanatic; he only has one idea.'
Well, it is a glorious idea."*

# CHRIST AND YOUR NEIGHBOR

"Go and speak to your neighbor and tell him
of Christ and heaven. You need not go far
before you will find someone who is passing
down to the darkness of eternal death.
Let us haste to the rescue!"

# THE FOUNDATION OF FAITH

*"Faith without works is like a man putting all his money into the foundation of a house; and works without faith is like building a house on sand without any foundation."*

## HIS PRESENCE IN ZION

*"It will not be the jasper walls and the
pearly gates that will make heaven attractive.
We shall be in the presence of the Redeemer;
we shall be forever with the Lord."*

# OUR FULL WORTH

"They say the Rothschilds cannot tell how much
they are worth; and that is just my case.
All things in the world are mine.
I am joint heir with Jesus the Son of God."

## The Finger of Scorn

"God cannot use you until you are willing to have the world point the finger of scorn at you."

*Rejoice, and be exceeding glad: for great is your reward in heaven: for so persecuted they the prophets which were before you.*

MATTHEW 5:1

## DID YOU KNOW?

When invited to speak at a special ceremony at the
church of the great preacher Charles H. Spurgeon,
Moody replied in characteristic humility that
he would also like to polish his boots.

# A LASTING MONUMENT

"*We can all do something for Him. It may be a small thing; but…it will outlive all the monuments on earth. The iron and the granite will rust and crumble and fade away, but anything done for Christ will never fade.*"

## Less Faith In Moody

"It is easier for me to have faith in the Bible than to have faith in D. L. Moody, for Moody has fooled me lots of times."

*Trust in the Lord with all thine heart; and lean not unto thine own understanding.*

PROVERBS 3:5

## SEPARATION FROM THE WORLD

"The church will have a convincing testimony and will become a power in the world when it is separated from the world; but as long as it is hand and glove with the world, it cannot have power."

## CLOSE UP AND FAR AWAY

*"Study the Bible with a telescope and after that study it with a microscope."*

"A good example is far better
than a good precept."

## Learn By Doing

*Verily, verily, I say unto you,
He that believeth on me,
the works that I do shall he do also;
and greater works than these shall he do;
because I go unto my Father.*

JOHN 14:12

## The Influence of Truth

"Don't you know my friend,
it is not the most fluent man that has
the greatest effect with a jury?
It is the man who tells the truth."

---

*He that speaketh truth*
*showeth forth righteousness:*
*but a false witness deceit.*

PROVERBS 12:17

# A PROTECTED FORTRESS

"Edinburgh Castle, in all the wars of Scotland, was never taken but once. Then the enemy came up the steep rocks at a place where the garrison thought it was so safe they needn't guard it... Hence, the necessity of watching and praying, because if you are not on the alert, you will be tripped up by the tempter."

## KNOWING THE SHEEP

"A gentleman in the East heard of a shepherd who could call all of his sheep to him by name…The man knew all his sheep by their failings, for he had not a perfect one in the whole flock. I suppose our shepherd knows us in the same way."

## *Learning Can Be Dangerous*

"An educated rascal is the meanest kind of a rascal."

---

*Knowledge puffeth up, but charity edifieth.*

1 CORINTHIANS 8:1

## THE CHURCH AND REVIVAL

"*There are the Catholic and Episcopal churches claiming to be the apostolic churches and to have sprung from Pentecost; the Lutheran from Martin Luther, and so on. They all sprung out of revivals, and yet people talk against revivals! I'd as soon talk against my mother as against a revival.*"

# LONG-WINDED PRAYER

*"Some men's prayers need to be cut short at both ends and set on fire in the middle."*

## SYMPATHY FOR SORROWS

"There are thousands of families that could easily be reached if we had thousands of Christians going to them and entering into sympathy with their sorrows. That is what they want."

## Praise God In Prosperity

"We can stand affliction better
than we can prosperity,
for in prosperity we forget God."

---

*Let them shout for joy, and be glad,
that favour my righteous cause: yea,
let them say continually, Let the Lord
be magnified, which hath pleasure in
the prosperity of his servant.*

PSALM 35:27

# A WORKMAN NOT ASHAMED

"Spend a month on regeneration, or the kingdom of God, or the church in the New Testament, or the attributes of God. It will help you in your own spiritual life, and you will become a workman who need not be ashamed, rightly dividing the word of truth."

# CHURCH OF THE GRUMBLERS

"There are a good many people that are always grumbling. I wish that we could have a great national church and call it a church for grumblers."

## *DID YOU KNOW?*

The Moody family coat of arms was given in 1540 to his ancestor Edmund for saving the life of English King Henry VIII. He was also a descendant of seven generations of Puritan forebears.

## A Kingdom Built on Love

"Napoleon tried to establish a kingdom by the force of arms. So did Alexander the Great, and Caesar,…but they utterly failed. Jesus founded His kingdom on love, and it is going to stand."

*And this is his commandment, That we should believe on the name of his Son Jesus Christ, and love one another, as he gave us commandment.*

1 JOHN 3:23

# MAKING HELL EASY

*"I want to be rich for eternity, not for time…
Short-sighted men accumulate
millions just to make the way to hell
easy for their children."*

# THE BLOOD OF CHRIST

"An aged minister of the gospel, on his dying bed, said, 'Bring me the Bible.' Putting his finger upon the verse, The blood of Jesus Christ his Son cleanseth us from all sin, he said, 'I die in the hope of this verse.' It was not his fifty years preaching but the blood of Christ."

## REACHING THE CITIES

"Water runs downhill, and the highest hills
are the great cities. If we can stir them,
we shall stir the whole nation."

"We are spinning our own fates, good or evil, and never to be undone. Every smallest stroke of virtue or of vice leaves its ever-so-little scar."

## Spinning Our Fates

*Be not deceived; God is not mocked: for whatsoever a man soweth, that shall he also reap. For he that soweth to his flesh shall of the flesh reap corruption; but he that soweth to the Spirit shall of the Spirit reap life everlasting.*

GALATIANS 6:7,8

## PARENT'S DUTY

"God's order is to the father first, but if he isn't true to his duty, then the mother should be true and save the children from the wreck. Now is the time to do it while you have them under your roof."

# WHEN FAITH HITS HOME

"A *man ought to live so that everybody knows he is a Christian...and most of all, his family ought to know.*"

## *DID YOU KNOW?*

It is estimated that Moody traveled more than one million miles and addressed more than one hundred million people during his evangelistic career.

# FALSE BLAME

"The best things I have ever done since I became
a Christian, I have been blamed for....Even
the religious papers attack me for the best things.
It is so hard when you are working for Christ
to have His disciples indignant
with you and say bitter things!"

## INCREASED OPPORTUNITIES

"The more we use the means and opportunities
we have, the more will our ability and our
opportunities be increased."

# WORKING BELOW

"No rest here below; nothing but toil and labor.
And you will enjoy your rest all the more when you
come to the beautiful land above. There are always
trials, and tribulations, and labors here.
Work on, hope on, pray on!"

## God In the Morning

"We ought to see the face of God every morning before we see the face of man."

---

*As for me, I will behold thy face in righteousness: I shall be satisfied, when I awake, with thy likeness.*

PSALM 17:15

# BIRDS IN YOUR HAIR

"*One old divine says, 'You are not to blame for the birds that fly over your head, but if you allow them to come down and make a nest in your hair, then you are to blame.' And so with these evil thoughts that come flashing into our minds; we have to fight them.*"

"Death may be the King of
terrors...
but Jesus is the King of kings!"

## The True King

*Forasmuch then as the children are partakers of flesh and blood, he also himself likewise took part of the same; that through death he might destroy him that had the power of death, that is, the devil; And deliver them who through fear of death were all their lifetime subject to bondage.*

HEBREWS 2:14,15

## *DID YOU KNOW?*

Moody failed his first examination
on Christian doctrine when attempting
to become a church member.

# THE GREAT MISTAKE

"I finished the sermon upon 'What Shall I Do with Jesus?' and said to the audience: 'Now I want you to take the question with you and think it over, and next Sunday I want you to come back and tell me.'"

What a mistake! Since then I never have dared give an audience a week to think of their salvation. If they were lost, they might rise up in judgment against me. Now is the accepted time."

## *DID YOU KNOW?*

He announced his marriage in print to Emma Revell
by merely stating he was no longer free
to escort other young ladies home after church.

# COME OUT OF THE CAVE

*"Don't imagine that you have got to go into a cave to be consecrated, and stay there all your life. Whatever you take up, take it up with all your heart."*

# PEACE ACCOMPLISHED

"A *great many people are trying to make peace, but that has already been done. God has not left it for us to do; all we have to do—is to enter into it.*"

*Straight-ening Grace*

"This law tells me how crooked I am. Grace comes along and straightens me out."

---

*For the grace of God that bringeth salvation hath appeared to all men, Teaching us that, denying ungodliness and worldly lusts, we should live soberly, righteously, and godly, in this present world.*

TITUS 2:11,12

# SOMEONE MUST DIE

"*I must die or get someone to die for me. If the Bible doesn't teach that, it doesn't teach anything. And that is where the atonement of Jesus Christ comes in.*"

# EXCUSING YOURSELF

*"It is easy enough to excuse yourself to hell, but you cannot excuse yourself to heaven."*

## NO TRIFLING MATTER

*"Never think that Jesus commanded a trifle, nor dare to trifle with anything He has commanded."*

## *DID YOU KNOW?*

Moody lost his home, possessions and church in the Great Chicago Fire.

# FIRST HAND EXPERIENCE

*"The difference between listening to a radio sermon and going to church...is almost like the difference between calling your girl on the phone and spending an evening with her."*

## Living Epistles

"Where one man reads the Bible, a hundred read you and me."

---

*Ye are our epistle written in our hearts, known and read of all men.*

2 CORINTHIANS 3:2

"Look at what He is, and at what He has done; not at what you are.

———

## Look To His Work

*Looking unto Jesus the author and finisher of our faith; who for the joy that was set before him endured the cross, despising the shame, and is set down at the right hand of the throne of God.*

HEBREWS 12:2

# THE TROUBLE WITH ME

*"I have had more trouble with myself
than with any other man."*

# LOVEABLE SINNERS

*God hates the sin,
but He loves the sinner.*

## Faith and Love Together

"Faith makes all things possible...
love makes all things easy."

_____

*And the grace of our Lord was
exceeding abundant with faith and
love which is in Christ Jesus.*

1 TIMOTHY 1:14

## *DID YOU KNOW?*

Moody's song leader, Ira Sankey, was said to be
as effective as an evangelist with his hymms
as Moody was with his preaching.

# DEAD HUSBANDS

*"'My husband is so good,' say some foolish wives, 'he lacks only one thing — he is not a Christian.' Well, all a dead man lacks is one thing — life."*

# THE CLOSENESS OF HEAVEN

*"We talk about heaven being so far away.*
*It is within speaking distance*
*to those who belong there."*

## Your Elder Brother

"You are no match for Satan, and when he wants to fight you just run to your elder Brother, who is more than a match for all the devils in hell."

---

*And if children, then heirs; heirs of God, and joint-heirs with Christ; if so be that we suffer with him, that we may be also glorified together.*

ROMANS 8:17

# THE BUSINESS OF PRAYER

"*If you have so much business to attend to that you have no time to pray, depend upon it, you have more business on hand than God ever intended you should have.*"

# THE MAN MOODY SAVED

A tramp, obviously under the influence of alcohol [said], "Mr. Moody, you're the man who saved me." As he observed the bearded face, bloodshot eyes, unkept hair, and torn clothes, he replied, "Yes, it looks as if I did save you. If the Lord had, you wouldn't be in this condition."

# UPPER AND LOWER LIGHTS

*"God keeps the upper lights burning as brightly as ever, but He has left us down here to keep the lower lights burning."*

## *DID YOU KNOW?*

On one occasion, Moody and one of his sons were nearly killed at sea. His son Will continued his father's legacy at Moody Bible Institute for over thirty years. His son Paul had a notable career in the liberal wing of American Protestantism.

## On the Side of Discipline

"It is better to be a little too strict than too liberal."

———————

*Foolishness is bound in the heart of a child; but the rod of correction shall drive it far from him.*

PROVERBS 22:15

## A *Vital* Necessity

"Church attendance is as vital to a disciple as a transfusion of rich, healthy blood to a sick man."

*And let us consider one another to provoke unto love and to good works: Not forsaking the assembling of ourselves together, as the manner of some is; but exhorting one another.*

HEBREWS 10:24,25

# IMPOSSIBLE TASK

"*I wouldn't think of talking to unconverted men about overcoming the world, for it is utterly impossible. They might as well try to cut down the American forest with their penknives.*"

# GOOD AND TRUE

*"God never made a promise
that was too good to be true."*

# PRECIOUS TIME

*"Sometimes a few minutes in prayer have done
more for a man than two hours in talk."*

## TEMPERED STEEL

*"I wouldn't give much for a man that hasn't temper. Steel isn't good for anything if it hasn't got temper. But when temper gets the mastery over me I am its slave, and it is a source of weakness."*

# UNCOMFORTABLE IN HEAVEN

*"Heaven would be hell to a man who had not repented."*

## DID YOU KNOW?

At the Chicago World's Fair in 1893,
over 130,000 people attended Moody's
evangelistic meetings in one day.

# THE FOOD OF GOD'S WORD

"Read the Bible itself; do not spend all your time on commentaries and helps. If a man spent all his time reading up the chemical constituents of bread and milk, he would soon starve."

## STRAIGHT vs. CROOKED

*"The best way to show that a stick is crooked is not to argue about it or to spend time denouncing it, but to lay a straight stick alongside it."*

## True Loss

"We know what it is to lose health and wealth and reputation...but what is the loss of all these things compared with the loss of the soul?"

———————

*For what shall it profit a man, if he shall gain the whole world, and lose his own soul?*

MARK 8:36

# UNIQUE EXPERIENCES

*"He never made two men just alike,*
*or converted two men just alike.*
*That is where a great many people blunder,*
*looking for God to give them*
*somebody else's experience."*

# RUMORS OF DEATH
# EXAGGERATED

"Someday you will read in the papers that Moody is
dead. Don't you believe a word of it. At that
moment I shall be more alive than I am now...I was
born of the flesh in 1837, I was born of the Spirit in
1855. That which is born of the flesh may die. That
which is born of the Spirit shall live forever."

# RECEIVE HIM NOW

"If you take the gift of God you are saved. If you have eternal life you need not fear fire, death, or sickness. Let disease or death come, you can shout triumphantly over the grave if you have Christ. My friends, what are you going to do with Him? Will you not decide now?"

Additional copies of this book and other portable book titles from Honor Books are available at your local bookstore:

*Martin Luther's Little Instruction Book*

*John Wesley's Little Instruction Book*

*Larry Burkett's Little Instruction Book*

*God's Little Instruction Book* (series)